I0753509
THE VENTURE
Letters To Those Who Come Next

Published by The Story Cure Press
Honolulu, Hawai`i

ISBN: Paperback: 978-1-970366-17-4
ISBN: Ebook: 978-1-970366-18-1

Printed in the United States of America
TheStoryCurePress.co

INTRODUCTION

At VALE, we believe learning should lead to something real. We don't just focus on grades or assignments that live in a folder somewhere, but experiences that ask students to think deeply, solve problems, take risks, and create something that matters to them and the world around them. **The Venture: Letters to Those Who Come Next** is one of the most powerful ways we bring that belief to life.

This project asks our first graduating class of seniors to pause and reflect on who they are becoming, what they care about, and how they want to leave their mark. Each project represents months of curiosity, persistence, and courage. Some ideas worked right away, although many didn't, requiring lots of iteration. That's part of the journey. Learning to navigate uncertainty, adapt, and keep moving forward is exactly what this experience is meant to teach.

This book captures those journeys.

Inside these pages you will see the ideas, challenges, pivots, and breakthroughs that our seniors experienced as they designed something meaningful to them. No two projects are the same, and that's exactly the point. Each reflects the voice, interests, and growth of the student behind it.

Our hope is that this book serves as both a celebration and a reminder. A celebration of the incredible work these students have done, and a reminder that young people are capable of far more than we sometimes give them credit for when they are trusted with real opportunities and supported by a community that believes in them.

To our seniors: thank you for your courage, creativity, and willingness to lean into the unknown.

Your legacy begins here.

Lee-Ann Hayen
Chief Learner & Disruptor.

Laura Burke
Chief of Innovative Systems & Empowerment

EDITOR'S NOTE

In these pages live the voices of students who stood exactly where you stand now—uncertain, curious, overwhelmed, hopeful—and who now stand where you will be in four short years, on the edge of something new.

VALE did not open until 2023. It began with just a freshman and sophomore class. The Class of 2026 is the first to ever graduate from VALE—the first to define what it means to leave this place.

None of us started here. Every single one of us spent our freshman year or even longer at a different school. We left behind what was familiar: the routines, the hallways, the people we thought we would grow up with. For one reason or another, we heard about VALE and made the choice to begin again.

Maybe, at first glance, VALE just seemed different. Exciting, even. But truthfully, that's not why most of us came. We came because something wasn't working. Because we felt lost in systems that didn't see us, or challenged in ways that didn't help us grow. We needed more.

So we took a leap.

And what you'll read in this anthology is what happened before and after that leap.

These stories are not perfect, and neither are we. They are messy, honest, sometimes unfinished—because growth is like that. They hold moments of doubt and moments of clarity, failures and small victories that meant everything.

If you are a freshman reading this, wondering if you belong here, wondering if you made the right choice—you are not alone. Every voice in these pages has asked those same questions.

And if there is one thing this first graduating class can leave behind, it is this:

You do not have to have everything figured out to be exactly where you are meant to be.

Welcome to VALE.

From the editor of this book, and forever a part of the hive,

Kat Kimble

CONTENTS

AUTHOR'S BIO

Amara Fantl

Hello! My name is Amara Fantl and I am honored to be one of the first ever VALE graduates. In school, I started the CLEAR Initiative, VALEsgiving, was StuCo "president", DECA president, the "Heart" of StuGo, and the mind behind the Bridge dance! I graduated early Fall 2025 to move out and work in Washington DC in the US House of Reps. After my gap semester, I'll be going to Georgetown for International Relations. But most importantly– I am a radical optimist who believes life is the most wonderful adventure.

Values: *ACCOUNTABILITY, JOY, CONNECTION*

ON EMBARRASSMENT

Preface: Feeling embarrassed is one of the only constants in high school. I hope these ramblings help someone face that, or at least see it from another perspective.

Dear Freshman,

If you go into Martin's room, pull down the projector screen, and take 5 seconds to look, you will see a large black smear on the right side.

Oops.

In the first week of the first year of VALE, Kendra and Martin told me to go up to the board to solve a puzzle in front of the entire then-sophomore class. In my excitement towards demonstrating the way the area of squares was exponentially growing on a graph, I took the expo marker and wrote... right on the projector screen. And no, the screen is not dry-erasable.

As you can probably imagine, my face turned bright red. I stood there, blubbering, in front of the students and staff that I was going to spend 8 hours a day with for the rest of my high school career.

In my panic to erase the smear, I actually just made it worse and turned a corn kernel-sized blotch into a dollar coin permanent stain.

For a couple of weeks after the 'incident,' I refused to look at the board in class. Martin must have thought I was suspiciously into analyzing a piece of gum stuck on my shoe.

But today, three years later, I look at that smear, and I smile. I don't burn in embarrassment, I just think it's funny. It makes me think that I have left my mark. Literally. I think this is true for most of us. In the moment, we are entirely embarrassed by a small thing. Later, we find we can finally laugh it off. However, for the time that we find ourselves still ashamed, that shame is agonizing and all-consuming.

In high school, it feels like you are constantly doing whatever you can to not feel embarrassed. It is an exhausting and tireless effort to make yourself seem exactly one way so as to not give others ammunition to talk about you.

But in my daily ponderings about what being a human means, I have realized that **embarrassment is just the fear of being seen.**

We try so hard to hide the blunders that we forget that the blunders allow others to know that we are also human, just as everyone else. In many ways, allowing yourself to be embarrassed in front of others is a profession of trust and vulnerability.

In class, I often would be loud, dance everywhere, or say things others would call embarrassing. I know any of my classmates would concur. But it let me be myself completely. It let me laugh off the little things, which let me pay more attention to the big things. It let me pie my friends in the face during VALEsgiving, trip on the stairs everyday, stain my shirt, and say whatever my heart felt in class (within reason). I got to enjoy high school and that is something many others cannot say they experienced.

Most importantly, by being so completely myself, I like to think other people felt safe being themselves, too.

Embracing embarrassment also allows you to feel comfortable making bigger decisions in your life that might be against the status quo. Most high school seniors are currently in class. Instead, I've graduated early, moved to DC alone, and worked full-time for my gap semester. Finding the courage to do this was not easy, but letting go of fear of judgement has allowed me to listen to what my body needs and respond. My body told me I needed to graduate, and it was the best decision I've ever made.

Of course, embracing this is a difficult thing in reality. It always helps to remember that people will often find things funny, rather than something to judge, if you're the first person to laugh at yourself.

Important note: to actually learn to be okay with being embarrassed, you have to create space where others can safely do embarrassing things. Laugh with others, not at them. Life would be sad if everything was that serious anyways.

All that rambling to say, if there is anything I wish my freshman self would learn, it would be to learn to love being embarrassed. If you don't, you will spend your entire high school career worrying about being judged and not on enjoying your experience.

So tomorrow, have a dance party at school. Wear something a little more weird. Do one thing that a fear of judgment has stopped you from doing.

There are so many other pieces of wisdom I want to share. Being able to be embarrassed is the foundational one, however. It allows us to take up space and live without others' expectations. Everything else comes on top of that.

I don't know what other advice you may need, but I'd just like to share a few more pieces of wisdom I've learned over the years that might make your life a little bit better. Other than embarrassment, here are my rules and beliefs for life. Also, a TLDR for those who don't want to read three pages about embarrassment.

TLDR; and Amara's Rules for a Radical, Optimistic, and Radically Optimistic Life:

- **You're not responsible for your first thought, but you are responsible for your second**
- Take the day off school if the weather is too nice (if your GPA is good and skipping doesn't just mean more work piling up)
- Apply to opportunities you don't think you're qualified for
- **All feelings are valid, but not all reactions**
- Apologize for the things you've done wrong, even the little things – it builds trust
- Go to the taco truck all the time, get the Asada burrito
- Everyone has a story you know nothing about
- You will meet no ordinary person in your life
- You don't owe anyone an explanation for your boundaries, but you do need to tell them what they are
- Explore all alternative pathways, no one's journey is the same
- You can connect with every person about at least one thing
- Write a list of the morals you live by, writing down your rules for life will help you actually live by them

- Send handwritten letters
- To have a village, be a villager
- You don't have to be good at your hobbies
- Don't assume that what works for you works for everyone else
- You don't have to understand someone's boundaries to respect them
- Read the news everyday
- **Your experiences are very different from your identity**
- Learn to cook
- Romanticize being inconvenienced*
    - Traffic is a chance to watch the sunset
    - Heavy grocery bags are a chance to work out your arms
- Feel the full range of emotions– be angry, be sad, cry. Then, keep moving
- Never judge communities for not having the same traditions as you
- Download the books app so when you feel like doomscrolling you can scroll a book, not a video
- Give grace to the past versions of yourself that didn't know better
- Ask questions about people's interests
- Always talk to your Uber driver, they have the coolest stories
- Sign-up for almost every VALE opportunity
- Understand how your political views affect all people. Marginalized people's livelihoods do depend on the person who is elected into office.

- Research ALL candidates for local, state, and national elections
- Vote.

**for non emergencies only, without expectation of brushing off actual issues. #goodvibesonly perspective doesn't give space to process and solve all issues. Pragmatically radical optimism.*

It is not easy to simply integrate these rules into life. For the most part, they require significant experiences in specific life things to resonate with you. If you don't resonate, don't listen to them. **Pick one thing that stood out to you, and consider following it more deeply**. The other things will follow. But always vote.

Life might be hard as you start high school. It will continue to be so. But, it will get less and less hard each year.

High school will feel long and short, action-packed and boring, more dramatic and less dramatic than middle school, and in general, very overwhelming. But just like every other person, you will get through high school. You will meet your people. You will find a job. You will build a family. You will do whatever brings you joy. You will live.

And often, you will be embarrassed.

As an adult, you will continue to find spinach in your teeth.

You will trip on the stairs again.

You will be a beginner in a room full of experts.

That's okay, because everyone reading this page will also go through that.

Just give grace, do what your gut tells you to do, and laugh at yourself.

Who knows if this helped anyone, but I had fun writing it. And isn't that the point of most things?

Live whimsically.

With all the love in the world,

Amara Sophia Rose Fantl

AUTHOR'S BIO

Anthony Lambert

I am Anthony Lambert, a Senior at VALE. My life is basketball! My goal is to play D1 or D2 basketball and pursue my degree in Finance and Business.

STORY OF ANT

I'm Anthony Lambert, a dedicated athlete who loves basketball and all sports. I'm competitive, driven, and always working to get better, both on and off the court. My goal after high school is to play professional basketball or become a successful financial businessman.

I remember sitting in History class one day. The teacher was talking about the world, and I was lost. I couldn't understand the purpose, the reason, or what I could do with this information. Until this moment, I used AI to get me through and yet every class, every teacher, every moment made me feel even less smart, able, or capable.

And then there was a light in the dark. I FOUND VALE. I found my small senior class and every person I met instantly got me. They knew my struggle and they did not judge me for it. They knew it did not have to be like that. They leaned in and told me that my experience here would be different. Not easier, but different in a good way.

VALE is a place of flexibility, openness, and leaning in. Everyone here tries to understand me, not make me understand them. I knew in my gut that I had found the thing that would change my high school experience. A little voice said "Take a leap. Take a risk." So I jumped.

On my first day, we didn't go over the syllabus or take notes. We were thrown into Immersion Week, where we were supposed to unlearn what school has always made us believe. We did that by getting on a bus and getting OUT of school. Kids were talking about their businesses, excited to "pitch" and I was terrified and excited. Instantly, I experienced one of the first moments of pride in my school experience. My ideas were good enough. My experience was good enough. I had something to offer.

Teachers at VALE do education differently. Instead of sitting at a desk for 90 minutes taking notes and tests, they want me up and moving, experimenting, pitching. We work together to solve problems and show what we know. For the first time, I feel creative. When I struggle or shut down or come late, they don't give up on me. They work WITH me. They meet me where I am. The flexibility has helped me feel like I can do this. Before, I felt like my teachers worried about their paychecks. Here, they do everything they can to help you succeed and be a better version of myself.

Now I am getting ready to move to the next step. If I was still at my last school, I would be quiet, unconfident, afraid of what others will think. Now, I am open. I don't worry about what others will think of me. I am a better communicator, I ask more questions, I can speak to a boss. I have learned that my dress, my hygiene, my approach, can shape how I show up in my job, at school, and on the court. As a black male, being professional is giving me a head start in a world that does not always give us an opportunity or can make an assumption about who we are. I want to tear apart their bias, the stories that a black male is poor, uneducated, not ready to be a leader in the business world. Now, I can do that because I believe in myself.

AUTHOR'S BIO

Brodie Fields

Hello, I am Brodie Fields. I am a senior at VALE, and just finishing up my last few weeks before I graduate. I love music and playing the guitar. I'm also a huge nerd who's probably watched most anime under the sun. After graduating from VALE, I will be attending Dark Horse Institution in Nashville, Tennessee to study music.

THE SOUNDTRACK OF HIGH SCHOOL

I've always been more sensitive or emotional then most guys. I never liked roughhousing around or getting dirty. I think this may have caused some frustration with my father, as my older brother was definitely a "boy boy" and being his only other son he thought I would be a fan of all the roughhousing and wrestling, but I would usually just end up crying and screaming. Despite me being the more sensitive, I played football from 3rd grade all the way up to 8th grade, and quit before I headed into my freshman year of high school.

I've never really been a fan of school, though. I think most of that stemmed from middle school, as those years were the hardest years of school for me. I dealt with bullying in 7th grade and even was hit across the back of my head by a teacher in 8th grade. The teacher was never held accountable. Though throughout my elementary years I dealt with a fair amount of bullying from others, as well.

This especially wasn't fun, as I would go from said school to football practice, where I would honestly feel completely incompetent compared to the rest of my teammates. I couldn't run as fast, I couldn't hit as hard, and I couldn't even get much playing time as the head coach's kid. This, along with not really forming any connections with my teammates, made my last three years of football especially miserable. I only really continued to play to keep that connection with my father.

After quitting football, there was a stretch of time when I wasn't really pursuing anything and I felt like I had nothing I was good at nor interested in. I felt useless, as if I had no purpose, nothing to give to the world, nothing to celebrate. It was around this time that my mental health really began to become an issue.

I had been wanting to pick up an instrument, as I got really into music towards the end of my 8th grade year. This interest particularly spiked as I attended my first concert after the last day of middle school. After that night, I knew that that's what I wanted to do one day. I wanted to be up on that lit up stage and drawing in a whole audience. I wanted to replicate that same experience that I had for some other kid in the audience who may feel just as lost as I was in that moment. I picked up the guitar about halfway through freshman year. As I began to start to play the guitar, I realized that I finally had a natural gift for something. For the first time in my life, I didn't feel completely incompetent in something compared to everyone else. I continued to play guitar as I finished up my freshman year and ended up transferring to VALE.

I still remember my first day at VALE pretty clearly. I saw a couple familiar faces from middle school, though I still had this overwhelming feeling in my chest as I knew nobody and always had a hard time fitting in and making friends. Making friends ended up being the least of my problems in that first week of VALE, as I was introduced to the concept of pitching, standing up and speaking in front of an audience and trying to sell them an Idea, Product, etc. During our first immersion week, we were assigned to give a presentation to an audience. I was too scared to even join my group up in front of the audience, to the point where I hid in the student lounge as my group presented. I didn't really realize it at that moment, but if I wanted to do this whole musician thing, I would have to learn how to be up in front of an audience.

As I made it to my junior year, I finally had some established friends, not many, but I at least had friends now. For once school was a lot more bearable then it was previously. I continued to pursue music and play the guitar and even had the best academic performance I've ever had in high school. It felt like my parents finally didn't have to stress and worry about me missing assignments for failing classes. For once it felt like I was finally enjoying and also performing well in school. I even helped run VALE's immersion day for prospective students and MC'd it. My mental health was the most stable it had been. I had been taking medication to help manage my depression, and this seemed to help me more than anything had in the past. I also had the opportunity to play live music during the vendorium that year!

During immersion week of my senior year, we were tasked to create and pitch a product to our class. If voted highest by your classmates, then you would go pitch the entire school, competing against the winners from the other classes. To my surprise, I not only made it to the finals but ended up winning the whole pitch competition! Me, the same student who hid away from his first ever pitch, won a whole pitch competition. To say it was a different experience from my first year would be an understatement.

Though my senior year didn't exactly continue the same as junior year did. I wasn't exactly sure why, but some of my said friends from the year prior weren't quite as friendly to me as they once were. This wasn't a new feeling for me, as basically each friend I had made in middle school through high school ended up switching their tone with me eventually. Though this one stung a little more, as it felt like I could never keep friends. This sent me into a bit of a mental health spiral as I couldn't help but feel viscously lonely.

The start of senior year wasn't all bad, though. I began to build connections with many of the juniors, sophomores and even some freshmen. I also once again helped run immersion day once again! Our music club also began to really shine, as we had the most members ever and got to run our own Halloween concert where we got to play live music! I slowly but surely began to come out of this spiral as I began to refind myself. I was even given a grant and accepted to a school in Nashville Tennessee to study song writing and music production. Things I don't think I would have been able to accomplish without the help of VALE.

I believe that VALE Academy is a gift and not a place that should be taken for granted. I have never been to a school with a more caring and attentive staff who truly admire their students. I believe that you, too, can succeed at VALE.

To succeed, here are some tips I'll leave you with.

- First off, LEAN IN! These teachers will do everything in their power to help you succeed, though as the saying goes, "You can bring a horse to water, but you can't make it drink."
- Secondly, ITS OKAY TO ASK FOR HELP! Being vulnerable and asking for help when you need it is not a sign of weakness or you being "dumb." Failing and retrying is all part of the process. I will assure you every teacher here is more than willing to grab a reached out hand.

- Lastly, BE AUTHENTICALLY YOU! Authenticity is my number one value. I have never once changed myself to fit in or shifted my options to fit a narrative. I believe this is the number thing I can leave you with. I believe VALE is a safe space for you to authentically be yourself. Don't limit it to just inside these walls, though. Continue to be exactly who you are anywhere you go, no matter what others may say. I promise you if you continue to live your life authentically, you will feel more fulfilled in every last thing you do.

Brodie Fields 2026

AUTHOR'S BIO

Dax Connor

Hello to all you amazing people! I'm Dax Connor and I am one of the lucky few to be the first ever graduating class at VALE. I'm a young entrepreneur, CEO and Co-founder of Atlas Men's SkinCare and Co-founder of Vero. I am a Public Speaker. I have a black belt in Ninjistu and Jujistu and have been training for 13 years. I will graduate in 2026 to continue my businesses. As of writing this, I am still deciding on a college. Most importantly, I'm people driven and always trying to bring out the fullest potential in everyone around me.

Values: *CREATIVITY, INNOVATION, PEOPLE*

INTRINSIC TREASURE

I

What does it mean to change the world? Maybe that's too broad a question. How about changing someone's life or changing your life, or even something smaller, like, changing someone's day?

Life is kinda like a bunch of Legos stacked on top of one another. Yeah that's right... Legos. Each little brick represents an experience you had. A moment in time when something significant happened to you. Each of you will imagine exactly how these Legos are stacked on top of each other differently, and they impact you, impact your emotions, and impact your decisions differently than the person next to you.

See, those Legos make up a good chunk of who we are. If we are to create positive identities, we should look to build foundations of positive moments in time. Let's call them yellow bricks. You want to stack many yellow bricks on top of one another.

It's the same philosophy with the buildup of emotion. For example, you're having a bad day. You woke up on the wrong side of the bed. Breakfast was bad. You stubbed your toe on the way out the door. And then you spill your morning coffee on yourself as you get into the car. If you just stubbed your toe, you would have been annoyed most likely, but inevitably moved on with your day. Let's call these bad experiences red bricks. If your red bricks stack on top of one another, no matter how small, you will reach a limit. Everyone has a point at which you cannot handle the buildup of the emotion, stress, or pressure inside you.

It is these little things that can create the difference between a bad and good day. With enough of each, you can influence how each day of the rest of your life goes. You can then broaden it. Take each day's worth of bricks and turn it into whatever color Lego you associate that day with, and stack those up to become a year. 365 Legos. It's the little things that our brains seem to let go unnoticed, but are essential to our well being. From your habits to your actions, the little things will end up deciding where life takes you in the end. So try to build your Lego set with your favorite positive colors, instead of negative ones.

Have you ever just stopped and taken a moment to appreciate another human being for who they are? I feel most of us have done this for someone we love. Someone we care about...

But what about the people we haven't connected with yet? That stranger you walked by just a few days ago in the corridor? I think we collectively take each other for granted. You know that everyone has feelings, thoughts, and internal stressors building us up and weighing us down, but you never really consciously acknowledge that.

I just want to highlight that everyone is in a state of being. Within that is a magic, I call it, of potential unknown. I'm telling you, within everyone there is this fire, a passion that you can help burn brightly. It's not even that hard. I have done it in 30 seconds, by asking a genuine question, listening, and then saying, "Hey, that's pretty cool." It's incredible what happens in that 30 seconds. A beauty of personality, gleaming through the clouds. Cracking walls that we instinctively build to not get hurt by one another.

If only we could truly see what impact we have on others, no matter how small. I know someone, an adult, who was told at a young age that he was a "lost cause" and would "never amount to anything." But every time other teachers would have sent him to the principal's office, this one teacher kept him in the room instead. This teacher showed that he at least believed in the kid. It is because of that teacher that this person went on to graduate college, get a masters, and build a family. From the rubble, he was able to rise.

A small act, each day, can single-handedly save someone's life. Think about that for a second. You, yes you can change someone's life, if each day you do something no matter how small for someone.

Finally, if anything else, I want you to take this away from my words. Always recognize and cherish the time you have with those around you. Time never stops, and although it seems obvious, it sucks when the time comes to say goodbye, and you will always have to say goodbye. So everyday I wake up and try to get the most out of every moment with my friends and family. I try to impact those around me, because unfortunately it can never last forever. Make memories you will cherish and always carry with you. So that when you look back, it's of joy and not regret. Everyone has something special to them, and it's those things that you'll carry with you.

-Cheers, Dax C

AUTHOR'S BIO

Ella Terrell

Ella Terrell is a senior in high school at VALE. She enjoys creating art and providing a safe space for those around her. After graduation, she plans on getting a job in the school district and taking classes at Arapahoe Community College (ACC) for early childhood education.

A WAY FORWARD

My middle school experience was a nightmare. I didn't fit in. I was bullied. But it was over, high school, a fresh start. My hope quickly dissolved, as high school began much like middle school; the bullying only got worse, and I continued to struggle to find my place. I realized that I was held to very little accountability at school, which only made matters worse. The result was my diminishing mental health, and I felt I had no choice but to do what made me feel good.

Now, what makes you feel good, especially in such a mental space, is not always what's really good for you. I began cutting class. Along the way, I met some people who were in the same boat as I was. Day in and day out, we began ditching classes together. What we did instead often landed me in the principal's office. A part of me knew I was only making things harder for myself. But at the same time, I was willing to do whatever it took to escape that low, miserable feeling, even if for just a moment.

Inevitably over time, my poor decisions began to put a strain on my relationships. I could see the heartbreak and disappointment all over my mother's face, and my father and I were at a near constant battle. The more I fought with my family, the worse my mental health got. I felt like I no longer had a space where I could just be anymore, there was always a conversation about how I could be doing better no matter where I went. Feeling that way only pushed me further away from getting help.

As I continued down this path, and got suspension after suspension, I was left with no choice but to transfer to another school where I could find more support. The summer came and went, and suddenly I found myself walking through the doors of a school for entrepreneurship named VALE. It was the very first year VALE was open. I was riddled with uncertainty, but tried my best to keep an open mind. Before I knew it, I was starting my Sophomore year, in a totally new place, with totally new faces. I began meeting new people, but I still held onto those old habits.

The relationships I was building were much like those in my past, and some of those habits led me back to the principal's office, but this time I was seen for more than just my mistakes. I could tell that the people I was surrounded by really did care about me, and it made me feel a guilt that I had not felt before. I knew these people saw my potential and wanted nothing more than for me to live up to it, so when I didn't, I felt disappointed in myself. Deep down I wanted to be different. As the year went on and I got past more bumps in the road, I caught a glimpse of the person I could become if I put in the effort. Just like that, another school year was coming to a close, but this time I felt sad going home, knowing I wouldn't return for a few months. It was summer yet again and I went on about my life until the next school year began.

My junior year didn't start the way I had intended it to. I was in quite a low spot at the time and began to lean back on those unhealthy ways of coping. A little before the second semester of this year, things started to really shift. I was making much healthier connections, and I began to realize that my grades were less about passing or failing, and more about the hard work and effort it takes to get something out of your learning. I started staying after school on Wednesdays to get proper practice and notes on math, and little by little, the work started to pay off. I went from failing nearly every class throughout my academic career, to passing every class including my weakest subject. For the first time, I felt like I had something I could really be proud of, I felt a confidence which I had never felt before. I learned that I was so afraid of failure that I had never allowed myself the chance to succeed.

From that moment on, I decided there would be no more hiding. I put effort into every class I had and ended the year strong. On the last day of school, there is always an award ceremony, and at that ceremony I was given the award for most academic growth. It was such a surreal feeling to receive this award, because I always thought of myself as someone who only did what was expected of her to get by, if that. Being called to the attention of a large group of people to recognise my growth and persistence was sort of astounding to me.

Another summer came and went, and I was on to my last year of high school: senior year. I went into this year both confident in my ability to do the thing, and nervous to begin planning what the rest of my life would look like after high school. I felt strongly that this year would have a lot more in store for me, and I couldn't have been more correct. Business went as usual for quite some time, my relationships grew stronger, I settled into my role as a student, and things seemed to be smooth sailing.

My challenge this year arose when we began preparing for life outside of high school...we started applying to colleges, and in a matter of moments impending doom began to set in for me. I realized that I had no real passions or talents, and I had no idea how I was going to make a living for myself outside of these hallways. For so long it seemed like the end was unattainable, and now that I was face to face with the finish line, I felt paralyzed by any decision I could make. So with that, I stayed undecided.

More time passed, and classes were going well. When the time came to get an internship, I was offered the opportunity to aid in a 5th grade classroom at Flagstone Elementary, the very elementary school I had attended as a young girl. Working in a school had never crossed my mind, because the narrative I had been telling myself from the start was that I was not cut out for school, I was bad at it and would never succeed. But for some reason, I jumped at the chance to help shape young developing minds.

After I finished my first day sitting in on this class, there was a shift in my feelings. Seeing the excitement spread across 24 little faces just because I was there was totally new to me, but it made me so happy. I thought to myself, "This is something I could see myself doing." Each Friday from that day on, I showed up as ready as I could to work with these students, and learn about what it means to be a teacher. This is just the beginning of the process it takes to claim that title, but for the first time I felt like maybe the time and effort would be worth it; that it might mean something to me.

I never thought I would be in a position where I was confidently directing a group of people, let alone young students. But since beginning this journey I've found that even if just for now, this is my calling and I need to chase it. While the road along the way has not been entirely smooth, in such an accepting space, I was able to realize that the person I was portraying was not the person I wanted to be. As time has passed, I've grown more into that person that I want to be.

Even now, I'm still learning what it means to show up for myself, but I no longer see my past as a life sentence. It's a reminder of how far I've climbed and how much strength I didn't know I had. VALE didn't magically solve all of my problems, but it gave me the space to grow into someone that I am proud of – someone who chooses differently, even when it's hard. And if there's anything I've learned, it's that no matter how lost you may feel, there is always a way forward, and you are always worth the effort it takes to find it.

AUTHOR'S BIO

Ethan Hanekom

Hello! My name is Ethan and I came to VALE in my sophomore year. I would describe myself as a dedicated, cheerful person. In my internship, I work with my mentor on real-world case studies to figure out treatment plans and possible solutions to mental health problems. I'm headed to Metropolitan State University in Denver to pursue a major in Psychology and possibly a double major in Social Work, with the ultimate goal of getting my Licensed Clinical Social Worker license so that I can pursue my own private practice.

FROM 0.8 GPA TO GROWTH:
A STORY OF ONE BIG WIN

Hello, my name is Ethan and I am 17 years old at the time of writing this. I will be talking about my times in high school, and how I would do things differently to make life a little easier for myself so you don't make the same mistakes I did.

I've never been good at school or turning in assignments or studying, and just surviving the day-to-day was a struggle for me. As a freshman, I ended with a 0.8 GPA. Then I transferred to VALE my sophomore year. At the end of the year, I got my final report card. I've never been someone who gets excited about or proud of my accomplishments, so I didn't have high hopes.

But then I saw it: *I didn't fail a single class.*

That was my first report card since elementary school without a failing grade. It sounds small to some, but for me, it was everything. That one "big win" completely changed the way I thought, and school became dramatically easier from there. My confidence skyrocketed, and my drive to do work went up. That momentum started me on a path to much better grades, which is what I get now. I hope this story shows you that all you really need is one big win to give you the skills and confidence to change your path.

Lessons for Making High School Easier

1. Stop Slacking Off: Don't waste a whole year.
2. Go to Class: Don't skip.

3. Study (Eventually): Just starting is the hardest part.
4. Take Opportunities: Find things you enjoy if nothing else.
5. Be Social: Talk to people because everyone here is nice.
6. Be Yourself & Have Fun: These are the most important for your mental health.

Your mental health is a massive, massive part of high school. Keep it in check, and don't be afraid to take a breath.

AUTHOR'S BIO

Jake Ponder

My name is Jake Ponder! I will be going on a mission to Brazil for two years and coming back to attend BYU to study finance. I love sports, friends, family, and I LOVE my faith!

HOW VALE HAS PREPARED ME FOR WHAT COMES NEXT

In the summer of 2026, I will be going to Feira de Santana on a two-year mission for my church. I will be leaving my family, my friends, and everything I really have behind for that time.

Every day while I'm out, I won't know what to expect. I won't know if I'll be meeting a lifelong friend or getting jumped that day, and that's a little frightening to me, but I will know my purpose and why I'm there. Throughout my whole life, I've been a member of the Church of Jesus Christ of Latter-day Saints aka, I'm Mormon.

Being a part of this church comes with people stereotyping you and constantly asking questions about why you believe what you do. Most of my life I've gotten kind of annoyed about all of that, but that all changed last summer when I went to Santarém, Brazil for three weeks with a group of kids who were also members of my faith. These three weeks changed my life completely. I learned to genuinely love my church. I saw how it's changed my life and how it has changed others. The people I met in Brazil I will never forget. They were so poor and had every reason to hate the world and whatever they might believe in, but still they wake up every morning with a smile and find things to be grateful for. I learned so much from these people, and they are one of the biggest reasons I'm choosing to serve my church. I want to go and help these kinds of people and give them another reason to keep on going.

But what does any of this have to do with VALE?

While I have only been at VALE for just over two years, it has still taught me so much. I have learned more than just textbook material. I have learned things that have prepared me for my mission and things that have helped me grow my business and in life. But the two biggest things I'll be taking with me for the rest of my life are: seeing challenges as opportunities and remaining flexible and adaptable.

One of the challenges when I first came to VALE was the new people. I was used to my friends I'd had since elementary school, and some kids around that, but when I came to VALE it was totally different. Every single person is completely different in their own way, and I've learned to find the beauty in that and love it. Without some of the experiences I've had, I wouldn't be as prepared as I am today to go on a mission and meet even more different, unique people for two years.

VALE has also taught me to remain flexible and adaptable. It seems like VALE is constantly changing and iterating and finding ways to make the school even better when you didn't think it was even possible! But with all the change, it has prepared me for my company, which I now own and run. While pressure washing and staining fences, so many things can happen that you would never think of, like a pressure washer blowing up in your face, or even a staining gun blowing up in your face, or a whole bucket of paint falling on the client's concrete because your silly employee sneezed and somehow kicked the bucket! But VALE taught me to be flexible and to find solutions, and I am so grateful for all of the opportunities it has brought me and how it has prepared me for my life after high school!.

AUTHOR'S BIO

Jamal Spriggs

My name is Jamal Spriggs, and I am a graduating senior at VALE. I am passionate about basketball, music, video games, and Avatar: The Last Airbender. I care about everyone I meet and make it my personal mission to try and play basketball with anyone who will play with me. I am always humming whenever I think or just to comfort myself. I am a second generation immigrant with my parents and grandparents moving here from Haiti. I am academically interested in the medical field, but if money was not as much of a priority, I would either be an actor on Broadway or a Melittologist (look it up). In my perfect world, I would just be a large bear in the forest eating salmon and sleeping.

BEFORE YOU CAN BLINK

The passage of time: such a strange experience. I want to take a stroll down memory lane and I would like to take you with me. My goal here is to showcase my learning over the last couple years by sharing my experiences at VALE and in life that induced the discovery of my values, beliefs, and ideals, and describe the process by which I did so.

Now I'm going to say the most cliche thing in the world, but it really seems like it was just yesterday when I was in 8th grade and my English teacher said, "High school is going to be over before you can even blink." I vividly remember thinking how long 4 years was and muttering to myself, "High school is going to last foreverrrr."

Of course I was wrong, which is strange because rarely am I ever wrong. But, either way, I blinked and just like that, I am a graduating senior of the Venture Academy of Leadership and Entrepreneurship. Passage of time-1, 8th Grade Jamal-0.

The road that I have ventured across has been quite the rocky one. My freshman year, which I spent at Castle View high school in Castle Rock, didn't go so hot. You could chalk it up to it being right after moving from Connecticut to a new school in the middle of the year, or perhaps the fact that I had no idea who my principal was nor did I have any relationships with my teachers. But in the grand scheme of things, it probably did not help that I just did not care about my education. I ended freshman year and began sophomore year with a 1.7 GPA (that's not great, by the way). That was the point at which disruption in my education was necessary.

So naturally, as soon as VALE showed up on the radar, I enrolled. Having already experienced what conventional high school was like, it took a second to get adjusted to the approach VALE takes with learning. I do not wish to dive into the intricacies of the curriculum, but to give you an idea of what the culture is like, I'll explain some of the things that go on.

The first culture shock to me was the fact that I was not only able, but encouraged to refer to my teachers by their first names. This is foreign in schools and always has been. However, it did not take away from the respect and reverence I held for them. Surprisingly, It did quite the opposite, strengthening the bond with my teachers, and allowing me to relate to them on a more personal level.

During the first week of the school year, named "immersion week" there was no actual school. Instead we did learning and activities that truly embody what VALE stands for (both figuratively and literally). The purpose of immersion week was to establish what the culture of VALE was supposed to look and feel like. There was lots of ideation, reflection, mindfulness, design, and creation. Already in the first week, my understanding of what schooling looked like was flipped over on its back.

That alone was one of the biggest principles that VALE stands for. Change and disruption from ineffective systems rooted in the value of tradition. I entered a space where my voice could be heard no matter how quiet. To clarify, I mean that my opinions had value no matter what, but the school is small enough that you could interpret that literally. I was seen and noticed by people even when I attempted to hide myself. Through this I learned how to recognize when I needed something, and speak up to find the proper accommodations. I also became more aware of the needs of the people around me, as well as the needs of the world as a whole.

As I continued through the months of sophomore and junior year, a lot of my values actualized in my mind. I have had a lot of long conversations with a lot of people about "good" and "bad" people. It is common for people to understand that the terms good and bad are used to everchanging standards. You might be able to boil it down to good people helping others, and bad people harm others. There is A LOT of gray here. What happens when a good person harms others or vice versa? Are they labeled by their most recent action? Does adopting a puppy outweigh mugging an old man? The labels themselves are harmful and unconstructive. I find it much more empathetic to instead say one is "a person that does good and bad things" in order to inherently separate the deed from the nature of the person. Of course, there are people who may be more inclined to harm others for a plethora of varying reasons. But labeling them as bad pushes a confusing and hurtful narrative. If you have not concluded it yet, I am a little passionate about this and I am now mildly agitated writing this as if I just engaged in debate. I would write a whole other book on this, but unfortunately that is not my goal.

As I stated earlier, my values have become solidified over the past couple years at VALE. Values are beliefs, principles, and prioritized ideas that you hold deep to your core, impacting your decisions, actions, and interactions with the world around you. Values start as small ideas that, when cultivated correctly, can flourish into a core piece of your soul. Oftentimes you don't even recognize whatever the value may be, and the spark can come from an infinite amount of different personal experiences, inspiring speeches, music, books, or even video games (I got at least one from Minecraft!). For example, some commonly known values are compassion, freedom (Eren), family, authenticity, wisdom, and respect. Due to values not all being black and white, people sometimes practice the same values in completely opposing ways. This, of course, can cause conflict just like all other social constructs in society.

While we are on the topic of values, I might as well say mine as it would be to the absolute detriment of this book not to talk about myself for two sentences. I mainly value freedom, compassion, and creativity. This is because I find that when I take time and effort to be skilled at something, it feels like I am soaring in the clouds. For me, it has been basketball, music, and poetry that make me feel the most free, as those are the things I am most skilled in. When you get the chance to experience sustainable freedom that does not harm others, it creates inspiration, fulfillment, and confidence in the soul.

One thing about me is I love love. A lot. And naturally, I hate hate just as much. This has always been true for me, and I believe that has led me to be more empathetic and sympathetic towards everyone I interact with. Compassion is the understanding of the pain and suffering of others chained to the intense feeling to wish alleviation of said pain.

Lastly, people were designed to create. Most, if not all, creatures on this planet use what is right in front of them, except us. We choose to create tools and trinkets with the resources we are given. We design and ideate using our most primordial instincts. Creativity is in each person's soul and the fact that each person can express their creativity in a completely unique way is beautiful.

That is the very essence of what my values and beliefs are and why they matter to me.

What seems to be the most effective way to attain this type of self-actualization is by tons of deep reflection in a space where you feel physically safe, mentally safe, and most importantly, heard. In this environment, it is impossible not to embark on the journey of self discovery. I believe that it is absolutely necessary for each person, especially each student, to strive to find their ideals, beliefs, and values. This is because when you have a clear vision of what you want the world to look like, it becomes your mission to accomplish that first for yourself.

I have seen that with all of my peers here at VALE, as well as in myself. As soon as I began my journey of self discovery and growth, I started intentionally building skills and finding coping mechanisms so that I could accomplish the goals that I am passionate about. In a couple months, I will graduate high school with above a 3.0 GPA. This alone is not something to brag about, I am well aware. However, I started as a complete bum of a kid who couldn't finish an assigned book from start to finish to save his life. Now I'm a student who cares not only about his education, but also about the impact that he can have utilizing the skills and credentials gathered in the process.

I am proud of the academic and personal growth I have demonstrated over the past couple years. Because of that, I encourage you to discover your values, uncover your ideals, and solidify your beliefs. It makes no difference what grade you are in, if you're even in school, if you are 8 years old, strive to reflect and refine who you are as a human being. Through that, you can be the change you wish to see in the world.

So listen when I, along with a bunch of other adults in your life, say high school will be over before you can blink. Take it one day at a time, and strive to be a person that does good more often than not. Love ya, bye!

AUTHOR'S BIO

Kat Kimble

Hi! I'm Kat and I came to VALE in my junior year. I would describe myself as an advocate dedicated to creating meaningful social change. As the president of The CLEAR Initiative, I work to advance sexual assault prevention, legal reform, and survivor support through education, advocacy, and community action. I'm headed to Western Carolina University to pursue a double major in Psychology and English, with the ultimate goal of attending law school and becoming a lawyer.

BETWEEN THE BELLS

A Collection of Poetry Written Across My High School Years

My constant throughout my life has been poetry. It became the way I learned to return to myself, to find something beautiful in the quiet spaces within me. The ugliest, most unmanageable parts of my life were reshaped into something I could hold, something that gave me a kind of peace I couldn't find anywhere else. What follows is a collection of poems written throughout my high school years – fragments of growing up, stitched together into a portrait of becoming.

The First Bell

High school doesn't begin with confidence—it can start with confusion, pressure, and feeling like everyone else already knows who they are except you. This poem is about that first moment of realizing you're expected to grow into something you haven't figured out yet.

The first bell rings, and I flinch like it knows me
like it's calling a version of me I haven't met yet
a stranger stitched into my skin
who is supposed to walk these halls with certainty

I step into the noise
but it feels like standing underwater
everyone else speaking in clear, ringing tones
while I hear only muffled echoes of what I can't be

The bells don't comfort me
They don't guide me
They just count me
period to period
moment to moment
like I am something that needs to be measured
instead of held

Between bells, there is a silence
that no one else seems to notice

It settles in the space beside me
sits in the empty chair at lunch
echoes in the pauses
where my voice should be

I watch people move like they belong to a rhythm
I was never given the notes to follow
like every bell pulls them forward
and I am left behind in the ringing aftermath
listening to something that already passed

The second bell doesn't feel like a beginning
it feels like being told again
that I am late to a life
I don't know how to enter

I try to laugh when others laugh
to stand where they stand
but everything feels like an imitation
like I'm echoing sounds
that were never mine to begin with

And when the final bell rings
it doesn't feel like release
it feels like proof
that I made it through a day
without ever truly arriving in it

I walk out with the echo still ringing in my chest
a sound that follows me home
a reminder that even in a place full of bells
full of beginnings and endings
I can still feel like something
that never quite starts.

Skinny

In high school, you may lose people you never thought you would. This poem is about losing one of my best friends to drugs, and what it feels like to watch someone you love slowly become someone you don't recognize anymore.

In the corners of a darkened room
Where shadows stretch and silence blooms
I find the ghost of who you were
Before the drugs began to blur

You were the rock, the steadfast shore
The one who always gave me more
A beacon in the stormy night
Your presence was my guiding light.

But slowly, quietly, you fell
Into a deep and hollow well
Where every promise, every plea
Drowned in a darkened reverie

The warmth you gave, the steady hand
Became a fleeting, shifting sand
And as you drifted far away
I watched your spirit go astray

Each night I hoped you'd find your way
Back from the haze of your decay
But the grasp of drugs, relentless, cold
Took the heart that I once knew so bold

The laughter turned to distant echoes
Lost in a maze of shadowed throes
And the person who was always near
Now fades in the realm of my deepest fear

I held on tight, though it grew thin
A fragile thread where hope had been
But the more you slipped, the more I cried
For the person I loved was lost inside

Now empty spaces fill the void
The dreams we shared are all destroyed
And though I reach for what we had
The silence speaks, so deep and sad

In every corner, every room
I feel the loss, the deepening gloom
For you were the anchor, strong and clear
Now just a memory, faded and dear

I grieve for you, not just the loss
But for the dreams that paid the cost
Of a life consumed by cruel deceit
Where love and hope were left to weep

So here's to you, the one who slipped
Into the shadows, cold and stripped
And though the pain may never cease
I cherish the echoes of our peace.

The Void and the Overwhelm

There are moments in high school when you can feel completely numb, and other moments when everything feels like too much at once. This poem is about that strange in-between space where you don't know what you're feeling—but you know something is there.

In the hollow realm where silence dwells
Where nothing lingers, nothing tells
I float through days in numbing haze
Lost in an endless, empty maze.

There's a stillness, deep and cold
A void where once my feelings rolled
No joy, no sorrow, none to keep
Just a quiet, endless sleep.

Yet within this void, a storm brews fierce
An overabundance, sharp and clear
Where emotions crash and tides collide
In waves that rise, then swiftly hide.

I feel the weight of every sigh
And yet no tears can even dry
A paradox of deep unrest
Where nothing's felt, yet all is pressed.

The heart is barren, yet it aches
With every breath, the silence breaks
A flood of void that's all-consuming
An emptiness that's all-consuming

In this paradox, I drift and sway
In shadows deep, where echoes play
With every heartbeat, every breath
A silent scream, a quiet death

The nothingness, a heavy cloak
A thousand whispers, yet no spoke
And in this place of stark divide
I feel the numbness far and wide.

Yet here, in this consuming blank
The overfill begins to tank
A restless void that never sleeps
A silence loud where darkness weeps.

So here I stand, in paradox
Where nothing's felt and everything locks
In the void and the storm's embrace
An endless search for a silent place.

The Scars of a Once-Loved Child

This poem is about how experiences can leave marks on you—some you can see, and some you can't. It's about growing up and realizing that parts of you have been shaped by pain, but those scars are also proof that you survived.

Once a tender bloom of spring
With laughter light and heartstrings sing
A child danced in fields of gold
In innocence and wonder bold

But time, it wove its silent thread
And shadows touched the bright instead
The body, once so pure and free
Now bears the marks of pain's decree

The skin, once soft as morning dew
Now tells a story, dark and true
Where tender hands that once were small
Are etched with scars, a haunting pall

The gentle curves of youthful grace
Are marred with lines that time erased
A map of sorrow on the flesh
Where once was joy, now silence swells

In mirrors' gaze, a stranger's face
Reflected back, a stark disgrace
The child within, lost in the glare
Of wounds and marks that linger there

The heart that knew the sunlit cheer
Now hides behind a veil of fear
And every touch, a reminder stark
Of battles fought in shadows dark

The scars, like whispers from the past
Speak of a pain too deep to cast
Of dreams that bled and hopes that waned
Of innocence that's left unexplained

Yet in this body, worn and scarred
There's strength that's forged and beauty marred
For though the child's light may have fled
The soul within has not been dead

In every line, a story told
Of survival, fierce and bold
Of a heart that still can yearn and mend
And find the light as shadows end

So though the marks may bear their weight
And memories of pain create
Remember in each scar you see
A testament to bravery

For in the echo of that child
In every scar and every mile
There lies a spirit, fierce and true
A strength that grows with each renew

The body's wounds, though deep and real
Are but a part of how we heal
And in the journey through the night
There's always hope and morning light.

Heartstrings and Asphalt

Sometimes, the place you're leaving is the same place that shaped you. This poem is about leaving a town I hated to go to VALE, and realizing that even the places that hurt you can still hold pieces of your story. It's about the complicated feeling of letting go—of wanting to run, but also quietly grieving what you're leaving behind. Heartstrings and asphalt is a turning point in my poetry, my poetry from here on out also became more positive.

In the dim-lit streets I once despised
Where every shadow felt unwise
I gather up my worn-out dreams
To leave behind these muffled screams

Yet as I turn and walk away
A somber fog begins to sway
Unraveling threads of something deep
A sorrow I can barely keep

The sidewalks once so grim and cold
Where weary tales and tempests rolled
Now seem to sigh as if they grieve
Their silent cries, a strange reprieve

For though this town has stung and burned
It's etched in places left unturned

And in each crack where echoes lay
A sorrow lingers, soft and gray

The faded signs, the dreary view
The endless noise, the sky so blue
Are more than just a bitter plight
They're pieces of my heart's own fight

I long to flee, to start anew
Yet part of me stays tangled too
In every frown and distant sound
A piece of me is still around

So as I bid this town goodbye
With tears that fall and hopes that fly
I find it strange, this aching tie
To leave the place that made me cry

In parting, I may never know
Why leaving feels like such a blow
Perhaps within this tangled skein
There lies a love, a wistful pain.

Echoes of Us

Even when high school feels lonely, you're never as alone as you think. This poem is about the way we connect with each other through shared experiences, and how even small moments of kindness can remind you that you belong.

In the hush where daylight fades
And the night reveals its shades
There's a murmur, soft and clear
A call for all who choose to hear

In the corners of this vast expanse
Where every heart may seek a chance
A single thread of kindness spun
Can weave us close, make us one

Echoes of us, in every breath
In the moments shared, we conquer death
For every soul that feels alone
Finds connection in the unknown

When the sky is draped in grey
And shadows dance along the way
We find our strength in each embrace
In shared humanity, we find our place

Echoes of us, in every touch
In the bonds that mean so much
We mend the rifts, the aching seams
In the unity of dreams

Across the borders, through the strife
In every heart, a spark of life
We lift each other, rise above
In the shared grace of boundless love

Echoes of us, in every cry
In the tears that freely fly
For in our struggles, in our pain
We find the threads that tie the chain

So, let the chorus rise and blend
In every voice, a timeless friend
For in our common plight and cheer
We find the truth that's always near

Echoes of us, in every song
In the shared hope, where we belong
For when we grasp the hands that reach
We learn the lessons hearts can teach.

Sunlight

This poem is about learning how to accept what you've been through instead of trying to erase it. It's about understanding that healing doesn't mean forgetting. It means learning how to carry your story in a way that lets you move forward.

In the shadowed depths of heart's despair
Where sorrows linger, heavy air
There lies a truth, both harsh and clear
A burden we must learn to bear

The past's harsh echoes haunt the night
A burden draped in sorrow's might
Yet in the shadows, quietly lain
There's a choice to ease the pain

Acceptance comes like dawn's soft grace
To touch the wound, to face the space
Where darkness dwells and shadows creep
And find a peace, though the pain runs deep

The weight of what once seemed too much
A heavy hand, a cruel touch
Now yields to the gentle hand of grace
That helps us find our rightful place

In the heart's acceptance, strange and sweet
We find a space where sorrows meet
And though the pain remains inside
There's freedom in the tears we hide

To accept is not to forget or erase
But to embrace the scars we trace
To find a way through night's embrace
And see the dawn in a different place

In letting go of endless fight
We touch a new and tender light
Where freedom blooms in truth's reveal
And wounds begin to slowly heal

The burden lightens, the shadows fade
As acceptance wends through the charade
In the heart, a space anew
Where grace and freedom find their due

For in the act of quiet embrace
We discover strength, we find our space
And though the past may still reside
We walk with lighter steps and pride

So here I stand, with heart laid bare
In acceptance, I breathe the air
A freedom born from facing deep
And in this truth, my soul shall leap.

The Part that Doesn't Break

High school will test you in ways you don't expect. This poem is about the quiet strength it takes to keep going, even when you feel like you're falling apart. It's about the part of you that refuses to give up.

There is a kind of strength
that doesn't announce itself
that doesn't roar or rise
like something heroic in stories

It sits quietly in the ribs
in the spaces between breaths
where everything almost ends
but somehow... doesn't

It is the part of you
that stayed
when everything in you
wanted to disappear
the part that whispered
not yet
when the world felt too heavy
to hold

Strength is not always loud
Sometimes it is the decision

to get out of bed
when the weight of the day
feels like stone

Sometimes it is the way
you carry invisible bruises
and still choose softness
still choose to feel
still choose to stay open
in a world that asked you to close

There are days
when resilience feels like trembling
like holding yourself together
with hands that are shaking
like building something new
out of pieces that were never meant
to be put back together.

And yet
you are still here

Not untouched
not unchanged
but still standing
still breathing
still becoming
something stronger than what tried to end you

Resilience is not perfection
It is the quiet refusal
to let pain have the final word
It is the slow rebuilding
the gentle gathering
of all the parts that were scattered
and calling them back
like they still belong to you
because they do

You are not defined
by what broke you
You are defined
by what refused to stay broken

And maybe strength
isn't the absence of falling
but the courage
to rise again
with the same hands
that once let go

You are the echo
of everything that tried
to silence you
and failed.

The Last Bell

Graduation isn't just an ending—it's proof that you made it through everything you thought you wouldn't survive. This poem is about leaving high school behind while carrying every version of yourself that got you here.

The final bell rings like a sunrise
soft, certain
not ending anything
but opening everything at once

We stand at the edge of something
we used to call "later,"
a word that once felt endless
now folded into the present
like a page we didn't mean to reach so soon

Caps lifted like quiet prayers
gowns swaying like chapters turning
we are no longer just who we were
we are everything we survived to become

Behind us, the halls echo
laughter caught in lockers
whispers tucked into corners
the quiet moments we thought
no one would remember
but somehow shaped us anyway

Every step forward
carries a thousand small beginnings:
the first time we tried
the times we almost gave up
the moments we chose to stay
even when staying
felt like the hardest thing we could do.

The future doesn't arrive
with certainty
but with possibility
wide as an open sky
unwritten as the morning

And we step into it
not as finished stories
but as people still unfolding
still learning how to carry
our own names
our own dreams
our own light

There is a quiet strength
in this moment
not loud, not perfect
but steady
like something finally aligning
after years of searching

We are not leaving ourselves behind.
We are bringing every version
of who we've been
the broken, the brave, the becoming
into everything we are about to be

And as the doors open
to whatever comes next
we walk through them
not empty
but full

of hope
of beginning
of the quiet, unshakable knowing
that we are ready
for more than we ever thought

AUTHOR'S BIO

Liam Chismarich

Liam Chismarich is an inimitably, perilously, irrebuttably handsome and creative practitioner of the scientific method – possessing an irrational ambition to learn, comprehend, and create with all the beautiful insights and functions our reality has to offer.

IGNORANCE AND STRUGGLE

Slamming open the sliding glass door to the back yard and stumbling through—trying to escape the terrifying conclusion I had realized—I collapsed onto the icy stone slabs in the path of my backyard. More aptly than collapsed, crushed: as though gravity suddenly became threefold its natural strength, and, rather than the earth lying beneath me, the directional center of gravity was placed upon me. Me, who could only ever constitute an infinitely small fraction of the world's sheer mass. My lungs straining to expand, I heaved the weight of the world through mixed gargles and sobs droning into the night.

I was immobilized by the thought that the circumstances present in my life forbade me from ever reaching my dreams, and that my own intelligence was not great enough for scientific discovery.

I was immobilized by events which I thought insinuated something about my capabilities, about what limited possibilities would probably lend themselves to me.

I was immobilized by the future–one that I had created in my mind, substantiated by a chimera of events selected in bias, sewn together with tenuous context and inevitably ending in catastrophe.

When I finally could stand, I rattled out a scream at the universe for creating me the way it did; concluding this skirmish between myself and my perceived reality. The conclusion I had made that caused the event.....completly irrelevant. It was simply something that would serve as the catalyst for me believing that my entire life was over. One of many catalysts that, in combination with certain self beliefs and the notion of a causal universe, would serve to create reasoning for the position that I would never achieve anything. That was my constant struggle.

I, like most people, believe in the virtue of science. Fundamentally, it is about applying the scientific principle – that one thing causes another through the interaction of matter and energy, which is determined by a set of mechanical laws by which the universe operates – to our observable world in an attempt to understand it. The nature of that attempt to understand is to bring absolute truth to our unendingly vast universe, and that attempt is very comforting. Our evolutionary advantage as humans is understanding and predicting the world around us. It has allowed us to make tools, consistently predict where food would be, adapt to environments through invention, and create civilization. Thus, it seems essentially natural that the categorization and mechanization of the logic and rules we use to predict the world comes naturally to us, and establishes itself as a pinnacle of our principle philosophy (generally speaking): if prediction is the human tool, science gives it logical authority. Yet, it seems that this predictive capacity, which has allowed us to understand the world scientifically, is also the crux of human despair.

Psychologist Harry Harrlow, in the 1970s, in an attempt to understand human depression, studied a close relative of ours: the Rhesus monkey. He devised an experiment to induce depression in monkeys called the pit of despair, in which he would place a monkey in a vertical apparatus with sloped sides, so that the monkey could struggle to climb out, but never succeed. After a few days of this, the monkey would eventually cease to move: not dead, but not trying to live.

Harrlow decided that this was analogous to the model of human depression. What truly was happening to these monkeys? They were able to predict the results of their efforts as fruitless, and thus gave up entirely. Even if they were to be given a new circumstance, and a new cage, they might still apply that prediction of fruitlessness, and fail to attempt anything. In this way, humans are similar to monkeys. However, humans have even greater predictive capabilities. We can think years, decades even, into the future, and we can do it using intentional logical structures that allow us to give credibility to those futures we predict. We are the masters of predicting in the absence of experimentation. That makes predicting and applying our logic to the world around us very comfortable. We don't need to take risks we know won't play out well for us, we don't have to expend energy on a strategy that we know will not be effective. Our choices can be more carefully considered, and they can be given a feeling of certainty by evidence.

These calculations are essential to our way of life, but they are also dangerous. Fear can drive humans to look for catastrophe in the future, and we are prone to weigh that danger more heavily than other options to keep us safe, and our evaluations become a confirmation of our bias: looking for evidence to support our negative postulations. And there will never be any shortage of evidence, as we can isolate and pick apart every second of every experience without contextualizing it. If we are programmed, like the rhesus monkeys, we will confirm that bias using the same structure, only strengthening that bias. This can become a horrible, terrible, vicious cycle.

This exact cycle was my struggle of catastrophizing, and it caused me to curse the world. It caused me to fall flat on my dreams. It caused me to feel as though I was constantly fighting reality. It caused me to assume I was crazy. I could not force myself to consider these futures as potentially false, because "What if they were right?"

This thinking– however all consuming and mentally prominent it may be– is fundamentally flawed. It is akin to putting your future, yourself, your hopes and dreams, on trial. With little emphasis on anything but potential danger, your psyche creates a court room with no defense, no jury of peers, just a prosecutor occupying the role of judge. It is not science, it is a kangaroo court of you and your biology's own making. This court says, "Why struggle against the immutable future when it will only result in probable failure?" It convicts our dreams of naivete and wasting energy.

During my time, however, I have learned that this is exactly why struggle is meaningful. Our dreams are implicitly possible. We are so ignorant of the world that we can never hope to predict whether or not we might achieve them. Thus, all we can hope to do is try. It is to battle our own biology, reaffirm that we, as individuals, cannot know the future, and pursue our unassuredly possible dreams that are the height of our potential as human beings. If our world is progressed and improved by the sum of our individual dreams and actions, and if the wellbeing of humanity is the goal, then that struggle is the ultimate functional moral achievement, because it is our attempt to defy our nature to better our world. Not to struggle against absolute impossibilities that have been considered fairly and scientifically, but to struggle for those unknown entities that result from our dreams despite their uncertainty, and to struggle against the unfair trial that occurs in our minds.

Thus, struggle, irrespective of its conclusion, has meaning in its principle. In this way, prediction once again becomes a tool of the dream, as its purpose is not to question the dream's plausibility, but to reason in an effort to achieve that dream. To know that tacit moral of the struggle, and to turn our nemesis that is prediction into an ally once again – that is what makes dreams come true.

AUTHOR'S BIO

Nashaun Golff

I'm Nashaun Golff, a senior at VALE who goes against the grain. I enjoy working on cars. After graduation, I am going into the Navy to be a mechanic on a submarine.

TRIALS AND TRIBULATIONS

VALE hasn't always been easy for me. I transferred from Chap, and I've been here three years, so basically most of my high school experience. It's been a mix of highs and lows. I've had my fair share of conflicts and tough situations. Honestly, a lot of that came from me just saying whatever was on my mind without thinking first.

I'm not gonna lie, I've said things that caused tension. But I don't regret it, because that's how I learned. I've grown a lot in how I communicate and recognizing how my words actually hit people. There were times I meant one thing and it got taken a completely different way, and that taught me real quick that it's not just what you say, it's how you say it.

I've also had moments when I didn't see eye-to-eye with teachers. If something didn't feel right, I spoke up. Loyalty and honesty matter a lot to me, and sometimes that puts me in tough spots—like taking the blame for things because I'm not the type to call people out. I'd rather be real than just say what people want to hear.

But I've learned that the way I say things, including my tone and my word choice, can either help or make everything worse. There were times I made situations bigger than they needed to be just because of how I came across. Now I get that if you actually want to be heard, you've gotta communicate in a way people can receive.

There were also classes where I didn't always see the point. If I didn't feel like something had purpose or connected to my goals, it was hard for me to lock in. Sometimes I pushed back or didn't put in the effort, especially if it wasn't required for graduation. Looking back, I can see that while I was trying to advocate for myself, I didn't always go about it the right way. Teachers aren't just making stuff up and they're trying to reach a lot of different students, not just me.

All of that forced me to figure out how to balance speaking up for myself with actually respecting other people's perspectives. I used to always ask, "Why? Why does this matter? Why do I have to do this?" And yeah, those are fair questions, but you also have to be open to the answers, not just stuck in your own mindset.

One of the biggest things I've learned is that your words have weight. You can say what you want, but you've gotta be ready to own it. It's not about popping off or proving a point. It's about saying what needs to be said in a way that actually moves things forward.

Taking accountability was a big one for me. It's being able to say, "Yeah, that was me. I said that. I don't regret speaking up, but I could've handled it better." There's a difference between growing from something and just doubling down and making it worse. Real growth is owning your part and doing better next time.

I've learned that you can't just say anything, anytime, to anyone. You've gotta know the time, place, and how to say it. Sometimes that means slowing down and explaining yourself better. Other times it means speaking up in the moment, but doing it with control.

And listening matters, too. Taking a step back to understand someone else's perspective doesn't mean you're weak or backing down, it means you're mature enough to see the full picture. You can still stand your ground and be real, but do it in a way that builds respect instead of tearing things down.

At the end of the day, I've stayed true to my values, which are loyalty, honesty, and being myself. That hasn't always been easy. And yeah, sometimes it has put me in tough situations. But I've learned that growth is about balance. You don't lose who you are, you just learn how to move smarter.

If there's one thing I'd say, it's this: speak your mind, but be smart about it. Adjust how you talk depending on who you're talking to. The way you talk with your friends isn't the same way you should talk in class. Learning that saved me from a lot of unnecessary problems.

But also, don't stay quiet just because it's uncomfortable. If something needs to be said, say it. Either you'll figure something out, or you'll learn something about the situation or the person. Just know there's a difference between speaking up to understand and speaking in a way that makes everything worse.

You don't grow by just going along with everything. You grow by asking questions, thinking for yourself, and challenging things the right way.

And probably the biggest lesson is to step back and look at the full picture. If you only see your side, you're missing half of what's actually going on. When you understand both sides, that's when you can actually move forward.

AUTHOR'S BIO

Reilly Mccoy

A quick point on my activity after school and my plans:

I plan to go to Abertay University in Dundee Scotland and study game design. This is to achieve one of my goals in life which is to create a successful game. After my 3 year college, I plan to return to the US and apply to jobs in the US ideally in game design, if things go well and I'll be able to apply to my dream job, a game designer for VALVE and hopefully find success there. There are higher goals I wish to achieve, but it's better to keep this brief.

About Reilly Mccoy, a collective of quotes:

"Reliable friend, great dungeon master, who also happens to be addicted to gambling." -Avery

"The most creative person I know, he's always there when you need someone to talk to or someone to win against in Magic the Gathering." -Levi

"A smol bean that makes better finance choices than his partner, and who is also quite creative." - KCB

"Hmmmmmm, a compass that doesn't know which way is north or south or east or west." -Mathue

"The man with the plan, or the desperate want for there to be one. Essentially, a decisive schemer, and a crafter, always making something new." -Liam

"Reilly is astute" -Martin

BARE BONES

My essay is about what matters and what doesn't. It's about how easy school is when you realize what you need to do, and overall how to succeed in school generally. In school and life, success can be built atop a future focused mindset, usage of the flexibility of mind and body, and the understanding that problems will resolve themselves with patience or active effort.

The first principle is: "future focused," which means that actions should be based on how it'll help you later in life. With the goal to alleviate future hardship though prior planning and set up. An example would be to establish a savings account as early as possible in order to grow your finances in order to cover later expenses, although your focus should not be necessarily financial.

The second is: "the flexibility of mind and body," which means that throughout your time in school and life, your body and mind are able to change and adapt to the situation. With much of the hardships being of mind and the remaining being of material. However you choose to adapt your mind and body, do so quickly and do your best to choose stable and reliable ways to change your mind and body.

Finally, the 3rd principle: "it will get better" which means that, despite the situation that you find yourself in, over time, the issues will resolve. A practice that shows this would be to avoid a potentially stressful situation by waiting for more information before acting or waiting for the situation to resolve itself.

The idea of "it will get better" also falls into two major categories, self resolution and active resolution. With self resolution being akin to being sick, the issue (being sick) will resolve itself with time, and thus patience is key. However, in active resolution, the problem in question will not resolve itself within a reasonable time. Active resolutions require effort and will resolve only with sufficient effort being provided. For instance, if you need money to repair your car, you must work in order to gain money to pay for the repairs. Thus, things will get better. It is up to you on how they will improve. Also, if you're reading this, I'm sorry.

With the principles defined, an aspect of success that uses those principles is the prioritization of school and what exactly matters in it. What matters in school, specifically, is school itself. It's the driving force for success in life and should take priority above many other things in life that demand your attention.

High school is the prerequisite for a majority of definitions for success. A definition of success is where you spend the most time doing things that make you happy. In this definition, you may need a job that can provide substantial income; many of these jobs require a high school diploma. Without a diploma, many positions may be inaccessible to you. <u>Prioritizing school is of the utmost importance, and is in your best interest to complete thoroughly.</u>

The second aspect of success is to understand what the future is based upon and to use that knowledge to your benefit. Understanding the future is difficult due to the various things that can change. However, despite the rapid change in the modern era, there are stable aspects. Knowing what is and isn't stable allows you to understand the future. In the real world, some colleges in the US are highly priced at the time of writing, this has been true for many years, and thus is a stable point. Knowing that college is expensive allows you to prioritize scholarships and funding for college. With that, understanding the future is significantly simpler than it appears. The practice of knowing history and current events with quality evidence allows you to predict what the future is based on and thus what it may hold. With that knowledge you then can decide what activities to do currently in order to achieve the future you desire. One should look to understand what the future is built upon to the utmost of their ability, lest they be blindsided by what it holds.

These key principles are derived from the experience of one student, Reilly McCoy, a Chaparral to Vale senior who was generally considered successful in school and career. However, if you are to take one point away from this segment, it is a phrase taken from my father: "knowing is half the battle", which means the more you know, the better life will be. So please read other experiences in this book, you may learn something that can change your life. Thank you.

AUTHOR'S BIO

Roman Perez

I'm Roman. I'm currently 17 and about to graduate in two months. Throughout high school, I struggled with addiction. While I have left that in the past, I have changed my focus and pursued a career in medicine. I will be studying at CU Denver in the Fall for nursing. Throughout my life I have loved cars, so I decided to make a choice and commitment to start racing cars at the national level.

PEER PRESSURE

Sometimes saying "no" is a lot harder than saying "yes." That's what peer pressure is pictured as, but in most scenarios I find this isn't the case. I know it seems like I'm going to talk about not falling victim to peer pressure, but that's not the main point of this page. As you have heard in the past, drugs are bad. But everyone talks primarily about weed and alcohol. You might have been taught about the addictiveness of nicotine, but not what it is really like to be addicted to either vaping, pouches, or cigarettes.

You may be wondering how I got from peer pressure to different ways of consuming nicotine. Trust me, it will all tie together soon. While you will be offered a vape either at school or outside of school, I would advise you to not take a hit off of it. That's how the cycle starts. I can't control what you do, nor do I want to since it is your life. But perhaps my personal experience will make you think twice.

You're probably curious about how nicotine makes you feel. I'll give you a first hand description. I would put it as a tingly feeling in your head with a lightheaded feeling to follow. For some people, that definitely pushes them away, and that's what I wished I did, but curiosity killed the cat. One hit started my decline.

Let me paint the scene. My freshman year, I was friends with people who didn't care about their future and lived in the present moment way too often. I went over to one of my friend's house to stay the night. This was my first time really hanging out with him outside of school. We were in his room waiting for dinner when he asked, "I have a vape, do you want to hit it?"

I hesitated a little bit and asked him what it tasted like. He said he couldn't really describe it since the coil was burnt. So I hit it, and immediately felt that lightheaded, tingling sensation I talked about earlier. I then occasionally kept hitting it at school in the bathrooms before class. Once it got to that point I ended up buying my own vape from a friend. Soon I realized that I couldn't go a full day without at least hitting a vape once, but I didn't think much about how it was impacting my mental and physical health.

I then switched schools, and during the summer I stopped vaping. I should have kept it that way.

When I came to VALE, I met my current friends who are very driven and supportive. I fell back into vaping, and this time I was also smoking weed with it. It really never crossed my mind what it was doing to my brain. But my friends urged me to quit. As of the time of writing this essay, I have been sober for over 8 months now. I can still feel the lasting effects, but luckily they are slowly going away. Still, I know I'll never be the same.

The most important part of this story is the people I met. They are the ones who shaped me into who I am currently, and I'm extremely grateful for them. They got me through struggles that I thought I would never get over. I cannot express this enough: **It is extremely important to surround yourself with people who are like minded but also different.** I know that sounds contradictory, but stay with me here: if there is no diversity in your life or what you do outside of school, everything becomes a little boring. That's how I felt my freshman year at traditional school. But at VALE, I never have a boring day, especially when I am around these people. While some of them party and live the stereotypical high school life, they find **balance** and respect.

Let me share a quote that has stuck with me for a while now: "The past is a place of reference, not residence." That quote made me realize that no matter what you or anybody has done, the past can't be changed. That's one of the reasons why the windshield is bigger than the rearview mirror.

Now I want to touch back on the peer pressure that I was talking about, and how it's not what it is portrayed as. Well, sometimes it is people trying to get you to do something that you don't really want to do. But I find those are the people who don't respect you or don't know you. Personally, I wouldn't hang around those people for long.

But there are different types of peer pressure. I'll talk about the ones I experienced. The fear of missing out (FOMO) is a big one, even though it isn't really classified as a type of peer pressure. Something happens in your brain when all the friends around you are doing something. You will have that curiosity to do that thing you're missing out on. For me, it was vaping because I thought at the time it was cool. Let me tell you it's not. If you're trying to impress your friends by vaping or showing off that you have acquired some type of drug that they have done in the past or currently do, you have fallen into the trap of FOMO.

Like I said earlier, you're going to look back and regret something that you did. But it's nothing to be deeply ashamed of, it's a learning experience. Back to peer pressure. I could go on for paragraphs about it. You will fall into it at one point, either with drugs, risky activities, or just doing something even though your gut is telling you no. Let me say: If your gut says no, don't do it! Sometimes your gut is wrong, but 90% of the time it is right.

Since you have gotten to this point in my story, you are either interested in what's to come next or have related to a part of it. So let me explain what you might expect when quitting. For the first days without nicotine, you're going to experience heightened emotions. Personally, I was more anxious, easily aggravated, had trouble sleeping, and my vision felt off. This was the worst part for me. Withdrawal made it extremely hard to quit.

But if you make it to the end of the first week, your cravings will start to dwindle. At this point, you will be able to control your emotions a lot better than before. Your sleep will improve. Your energy levels will rise. Your overall mental wellbeing will prove.

By the second week, your cravings should be mostly gone. But watch out! Although this is the point where some people claim to have quit, it's nowhere near over. If you see a vape, your cravings may come back for a short period of time. Have the self control and discipline to not hit the vape!

For those of you looking for tips, the most helpful one I found was to get a bag of Jolly Ranchers and suck on those to calm your cravings. It also helps to join a support group and keep yourself busy with other activities that you enjoy. While everyone's withdrawal symptoms will be a little different, most of the people I have talked to about quitting experienced this.

They did it. I did it. You can do it, too.

r

AUTHOR'S BIO

William Everett

William Everett is a senior at VALE and founder of the Blood on the Clocktower Club. He hosts games of Blood on the Clocktower every Wednesday and rides the light rail into Denver for his internship every Tuesday and Thursday. After graduation, William plans to attend Vancouver Film School in British Columbia for Game Design.

WE CAN DO HARD THINGS

Intro

Hi my name is William Everett. I don't know how much you've already read, what you've read about, or if you even give a [Darn] about this book. I don't know what kind of person you are, your hobbies or interests, your struggles or pains, or even your name. But I do know that you're likely reading this because you were told to.

I'm writing about mental health. I'm of the belief that talking about and reflecting on mental health is most effective when it's voluntary. It's important to me that if you read my section, that you are both comfortable with the material and you want to be reading it. This section contains discussion and rarely vague description of Suicide, Verbal, Emotional, and Physical Abuse, and Sexual Assault. That being said, if you are or ever become uncomfortable reading this section, if you don't think now is a healthy time for you to be reading this section, or if you think reading this section will be more helpful for you in the future, then I implore you to talk with a trusted adult and work out a plan that works for both of you.

For those of you who know you're perfectly capable of reading this section and are only seeing this as the perfect opportunity to worm your way out of some work, I ask just one thing from you. I want you to skim the rest of this section as quickly or as slowly as you want. As you're skimming, I want you to find a sentence that catches your eye. You don't have to do anything with it, you don't have to write a reflection on why it caught your eye, you don't even have to read it. After that, you can decide when you're done reading this section.

Part One: I Didn't Think I Would Live to See High School

Back in sixth grade, I was hospitalized for the first time. I've since been inpatient two other times, been in a Partial Hospitalization Program around four times, been in Intensive Out Patient at least twice, and had enough psychological evaluations to lose count.

In seventh grade, I was doing online school. I never left the house and had almost no social interaction. But something good did happen. I discovered a game called "Splatoon" and it quickly became my special interest.

In eighth grade, I spent the whole year an anxious mess after my guidance counselor misinterpreted my trauma response as me having been sexually assaulted. This is a complicated story that deserves to be told by everyone involved, but unfortunately I can only give my personal perspective.

When I was younger, I had this friend who lived just down the street. Let's call him "Neighbor Kid" or NK for short. We were so young when we met that I don't remember it. We would hang out often, playing video games and building Legos, until about fifth grade when I stopped being friends with him.

Whenever we hung out, NK showed some abusive tendencies. He often spit on me. One time, he threatened to hurt me if I didn't say a swear word. Sometimes he would try to convince me that he was moving away to make me sad. But what stands out to me is that every time I stayed over for dinner, his mom made us wash our hands using the bathroom sink. And every time I washed my hands, he would first try to convince me that the handles for the hot and cold water had been switched. When that didn't work, he would wait until my hands were in the water and he'd set the water as hot as possible and laugh when I burned my hands.

From what I saw of NK's home life, I would describe his relationship with his mom as tense. There was this cycle between me, NK, and NK's mom. When NK acted out and pushed my boundaries, I would go to his mom. His mom would often use physical discipline to try and correct his behavior. He would come back from the garage crying, and we would go back to playing.

It never worked. The behavior continued and the cycle would repeat. There was one time he was so desperate for me not to go upstairs to tell his mom that he resorted to trying to drag me back down into the play room.

When NK touched me inappropriately, it was the straw or rather the steel pipe that broke the camel's back. Years of being treated like crap culminated in me finally confronting and breaking things off with NK.

As you might expect, my experiences with NK have left me with a lot to work through in therapy and impacted me in a lot of different ways.

One day about half way through 8th grade, the kid sitting next to me accidentally brushed the end of his pencil across my arm a few times. For whatever reason, this triggered me and I had a breakdown. Once I was in the counselor's office, the counselor had somehow come to the conclusion that I had been sexually assaulted by my classmate (at no point have I believed this to be true). My classmate had his schedule completely changed so that we didn't share any classes and the rumors and gossip got really bad. I spent the rest of the year feeling anxious and having intrusive thoughts about my classmate and his friends trying to get revenge.

Throughout middle school, I struggled to imagine myself making it to ninth grade. I was in the counseling office all the time and getting a psych eval about every two months. I once had a manic episode near the end of a class, so during the passing period I walked around the building instead of going to my next class. Then I felt guilty, so I walked myself into the office and asked them to give me detention for "skipping class." My mom had to pay me to go to school. I felt like the only reason to keep living was because other people wanted me to.

Overall my experience with middle school was really darn bad, and I wouldn't be surprised if yours was, too.

Part Two: Freshman Year

I know you're probably expecting this to be the part where I talk about how when I got to VALE, I was saved by all the puppies and rainbows and my whole life was better and I was finally happy. But the thing is, VALE didn't exist during my freshman year.

My freshman year started off with two good things happening. The first good thing was the Splatoon 3 release. Words cannot express how much I love this game and how much it's changed my life for the better. The second good thing was that I apologized to my classmate from 8th grade. His response was something along the lines of, "Oh yeah, it's fine. I don't care." But let me tell you, I didn't realize how literal the expression "the weight lifted off my shoulders" was until that moment.

After those two good things, the rest of freshman year was a moderate to severe dumpster fire. Making it to high school after so much doubt was an accomplishment completely overshadowed by the overwhelming dread of making it to high school. I'm pretty sure the only classes I passed were Robotics and Intro to Game Design. Socially, I didn't feel like I fit well with any of the friend groups I hung around. I'd done all of the things I wanted to do with my life and had a strong desire to lie in a ditch and wait to die.

Near the end of the year, my intrusive thoughts got really bad and I was hospitalized for the second time. I spent the rest of the year doing Edgenuity in the library instead of going to class. Freshman year was probably my rock bottom. I constantly wanted to die and the only thing I had to look forward to was three more years of constantly wanting to die.

Part Three: VALE

So this when the puppies and rainbows show up right?

No.

Unfortunately sophomore year was still pretty rough and junior year was a little harder. Don't get me wrong, VALE is the best school I've ever gone to and I truly believe it's saved my life. I passed all my classes and made up for a bunch of credits I missed freshman year.

Academically, I was doing the best I'd ever been. But during sophomore year (around the same time as freshman year), I had to go through another Partial Hospitalization Program. At the start of junior year, I was hospitalized for the third time.

But something changed for me senior year. Over the summer, I discovered a social deduction game called Blood on the Clocktower. It quickly became a hyper fixation and later a second special interest. If I tried to explain Blood on the Clocktower here it would completely take over this writing, so if you're curious enough just google it. I think Blood on the Clocktower is the best thing to ever happen to my social life and it might just be the best thing to happen to me at all. In short, this game gave me the ability to call people my friends. Before now, I had people I talked with but I felt like I didn't have any connections strong enough for me to justify calling them my friends. But now I play games of Blood on the Clocktower with 7-13 other people after school every Wednesday. Senior year has been the best year of school I've ever had.

Part Four: Conclusion

So what do I think your main takeaway should be?

GET A SOCIAL LIFE

and YOU ARE MORE CAPABLE THAN ANYONE KNOWS!!!

VALE has given me everything I could possibly need academically, but VALE couldn't give me what made the biggest difference for me: the Magic of Friendship. But in all seriousness, you are the only one who can get yourself friends. In my opinion, it's the most important area to keep healthy.

Not a single person knows for a fact what you are or are not capable of. I've told you a lot of personal history that doesn't directly impact you, but I did that to show you how little power the past holds over you. I had to limit how much I wrote about the good things for fear of not completing this project on time. For every word I used to talk about my past, I could use a hundred times more to talk about how much my life has improved and it wouldn't be enough.

www.ingramcontent.com/pod-product-compliance
Lightning Source LLC
LaVergne TN
LVHW010836120826
845149LV00017B/1476